# FIELD GUIDE

*to the*

# NORTH AMERICAN
# BISON

*A natural history and viewing guide
to the Great Plains buffalo*

Robert U. Steelquist

**SASQUATCH BOOKS**
SEATTLE

Printed in the United States of America.
Distributed in Canada by Raincoast Books Ltd.
02 01 00 99 98    5 4 3 2 1

Cover design and illustration: Dugald Stermer
Interior illustrations: Jim Hays

**Library of Congress Cataloging in Publication Data**

Steelquist, Robert.
    Field guide to the North American bison : a natural history and viewing guide to the Great Plains buffalo / Robert U. Steelquist.
        p.        cm.—(Sasquatch field guide series)
    Includes bibliographical references (p.   ).

    1. American bison.  I. Title.  II. Series.
QL737.U53S698    1998
599.64'3'097—dc21                                        97-51773

Sasquatch Books
615 Second Avenue
Seattle, Washington 98104
(206) 467-4300
books@sasquatchbooks.com
http://www.sasquatchbooks.com

*Sasquatch Books publishes high-quality adult nonfiction and children's books related to the Northwest (Alaska to San Francisco). For more information about our titles, contact us at the address above, or view our site on the World Wide Web.*

# Contents

# Acknowledgments

This book would not have been possible without the assistance of many. Joan Gregory's curiosity and skill as an editor improved the manuscript greatly. David Gordon, Doug Chadwick, and Susan Ewing were enthusiastic in their encouragement. Pat Jameson, Ron Terry, Cheryl Matthews, Mark Heckert, Lana Safratowich, Wybo Vanderschuit, and Jeanne-Marie Souvigney shared important sources of information. For the times we have spent together on the buffalo trail that have made our lives richer, I dedicate this book to my sons, Daniel and Peter, and to my wife, Jenny.

# Introduction

Few animals conjure the power and symbolism of the North American bison. Painted on a Lakota tepee, minted on a 1913 nickel, or emblazoned on a poster for a Wild West show, the image of the buffalo stirs in us deep loyalties to the North American land, to something we experience as vital, wild, and part of our heritage.

Like most people, I have been aware of bison most of my life. I've seen them as docile brown lumps in zoos or as novelties in somebody's cow pasture; known they were "important" to Plains Indians; felt badly about their near-extinction, thinking it typical human stupidity; and celebrated news of their recovery as mild proof that people learn from their mistakes. But these bison have always been "symbol" bison—domesticated creatures or stone-dead images that served as shorthand for thoughts about the past.

None of these experiences prepared me for my first encounter with real, wild bison—a herd several miles away from me, surrounded by the broad shoulders of the high Plains. They moved almost imperceptibly, grazing on wild prairie grasses beneath a leaden sky. In that moment, bison came alive for me.

We moved closer to each other. I began to distinguish differences among the bulls, heifers, cows, and calves. They were arranged in small groups—a bull paired to a cow, a large calf hungrily butting its mother, a loose group of watchful outlying bulls, an old cow with a few followers. They communicated with one another using low grunts. Their movements had a rhythm, perceptible when I saw them as a herd. The land where they were seemed more alive, and I felt more alive in their presence.

My hope with this book is that it will help others see and understand wild bison in this way—in a way that will renew and enrich their experiences of our place on Earth and remind them of our profound responsibility to that place. By observing wild bison in their natural habitats, we can learn about their behavior and gain a

greater appreciation and understanding of them. And we can learn to be watchful that herds of free-roaming bison are protected, that they are granted the space they need not only to survive but to thrive.

Why should we care about wild buffalo? Because they belong to us in a fundamental way. That they survived their near-extinction a century ago doesn't lessen our obligation, now, to carry them into a new century as a wild legacy for future generations.

# Bison or Buffalo?

"Bison" and "buffalo" are both names for the wild relative of the ox that has lived on the Great Plains of North America since the ice age. "Bison" is the scientific name, referring to both genus and species: *Bison bison*. The term "buffalo," however, has been in common use for about 200 years, probably originating from *les boeufs*, French for beef cattle or oxen.

Because both words effectively communicate the image of the animal, they are used interchangeably throughout this book. Purists may insist on "bison" as the proper way to distinguish between *Bison* and other oxlike relatives, including *Bubalus* (South Asian water buffalo) and *Syncerus* (African Cape buffalo). Still, "buffalo" is the word we've come to associate with the symbol of the Great Plains: the animal made nearly extinct by settlement of the West, and the ecological centerpiece of the grassland animal community. Leave the debate to the experts—both "bison" and "buffalo" sufficiently convey our meaning when we discuss these animals.

# THE BISON FAMILY TREE

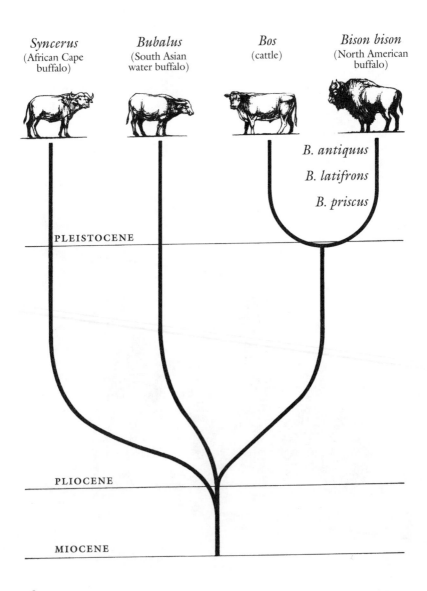

Syncerus (African Cape buffalo)

Bubalus (South Asian water buffalo)

Bos (cattle)

Bison bison (North American buffalo)

B. antiquus

B. latifrons

B. priscus

PLEISTOCENE

PLIOCENE

MIOCENE

# The Evolving Bison

The modern genus *Bison* is divided into two species: *Bison bonasus* (the European bison, or wisent) and *Bison bison* (the North American bison). Both are fragments of an evolutionary tapestry that spans millions of years and the geography of most of the Northern Hemisphere.

The first cowlike mammal, or bovid, appeared about 22 million years ago in what is now Europe. For the next 17 million years, bovids evolved into many forms familiar to us today: sheep, goats, gazelles, true antelopes, cattle, bison, and "true" buffalo. About 5 million years ago, the evolutionary line of bison and cattle separated from the line that produced the modern African Cape and South Asian water buffalo, which have broad horn sheaths, wide hooves, and habitat preferences different from those of bison and cattle.

Beginning about 1.8 million years ago, the bison branch diverged from that of cattle and oxen. Cattle were generally better suited to temperate, moist habitats near the equator; bison were well matched for colder, more arid regions. With the exposure of the Bering land bridge, bison and other Eurasian mammals migrated from Asia to North America.

Fossil records indicate that several early species of bison occupied various parts of North America simultaneously. One was *Bison priscus*, the "steppe wisent," widespread in both Europe and North America until late in the last glacial period. Ancient humans knew the wisent well; its image adorns many European cave paintings. In 1979, the mummified, 36,000-year-old carcass of a steppe wisent was unearthed from permafrost in Alaska.

Bison bison

Another early form of North American bison was *Bison latifrons*, the largest known bison, with horns that measured up to nine feet, tip to tip. Its range extended across the middle latitudes of the United States. It probably survived only until about 20,000 years ago, when it and a host of other Pleistocene giants vanished.

As the mosaic of habitats shifted with global warming, *Bison antiquus*, the "antique bison," achieved dominance, becoming the most widespread of North American bison and the first direct ancestor closely identified with modern bison. *B. antiquus* roamed from Alaska to Nicaragua, California to the Ohio Valley. In North America, fossils of the antique bison show evidence of human hunting.

Certain regional populations of *B. antiquus* gave rise to a subspecies, *B. antiquus occidentalis*. About 4,000 to 5,000 years ago, the modern North American buffalo, *Bison bison*, evolved directly from *B. a. occidentalis*.

For thousands of years, *Bison bison* flourished on the broad grasslands of the north and central Great Plains. Its range extended north into Canada, west into the Rockies, and east into the meadowlands and river valleys along the Atlantic coast. Northern and mountain stocks of *B. bison* further evolved into the subspecies *B. bison athabascae*, or "wood buffalo," the largest living bison. By the time European settlers began arriving, an estimated 50 to 100 million bison roamed the continent, the dominant species of the plains.

With their settlement of North America, European-Americans nearly brought the evolution of the bison to a complete halt. Altering bison habitat and systematically hunting and killing the animals

Bison latifrons

in mass numbers, they reduced the population to about 1,000 by 1889. The handful of bison that survived, forming the "seed herds" of today's bison, represented a wide geographical range and genetic variability. Further human interference, such as cross-breeding, the introduction of cattle diseases, and artificial selection of ranch bison, continues to affect the evolutionary development of the bison.

# Bison Distribution

By some estimates, bison occupied their maximum range in North America sometime around 1600, inhabiting grasslands, sparsely forested rangelands, and meadows in parts of all 48 states except Arizona and the New England states. In addition, they occupied parts of what is now northern Mexico, all of modern Alberta, and parts of Saskatchewan, Manitoba, British Columbia, and the Northwest Territories. Their greatest concentration was in the Great Plains.

The challenge of estimating the presettlement bison population was addressed by Ernest Tompson Seton, a turn-of-the-century natural-ist and writer. Seton estimated the full range of bison to be 3 million square miles. Comparing the grass needs of bison with those of do-mestic cattle and sheep, as well as the differences in how much grass is available in major types of habitat, Seton concluded that bison numbered about 75 million before white men entered their world. At the end of the 19th century, after the near-extinction of the buf-falo, what few small herds remained were in Montana, Wyoming, and northern Alberta.

Today, there are approximately 200,000 bison in North America, most of them in managed and ranched herds. The only wild buffalo of direct descent from the original plains herds are in Yellowstone National Park. Canadian herds of wild wood bison and plains bison occur in the Yukon Territory, the Northwest Territories, and Al-berta. Managed public herds of between 150 and 500 bison are scattered throughout the Great Plains, in various parks and wildlife refuges. (For a complete listing of where to see bison today, refer to "Bison Viewing Areas," page 39.)

Bison are ranched in all 50 states (including Hawaii) and in all Canadian provinces. A few large operations run between 2,500 and 3,000 animals; the vast majority of bison ranches run fewer than 500 head.

## Bison Facts

### SIZE

Males, to 2,000 pounds (900 kg); about 6 feet at the shoulder

Females, to 1,400 pounds (600 kg); about 5½ feet at the shoulder

Calves, 25–40 pounds (11–18 kg) at birth

A one-year-old weighs about 350 pounds (150 kg)

### PHYSIQUE

Bison have very broad heads and humped shoulders, which suits them well for feeding in deep snow. Long, dark hair on their

heads and shoulders adds to the massive appearance of their upper bodies. In contrast, their hindquarters appear undersized.

The hump consists of heavy muscles that are attached to the long bones of the vertebrae between the shoulders. These muscles and bones support the neck and head. Because of their humps, bison cannot roll over completely.

Males are larger than females.

Calves are larger than beef calves, with higher shoulders and shorter necks.

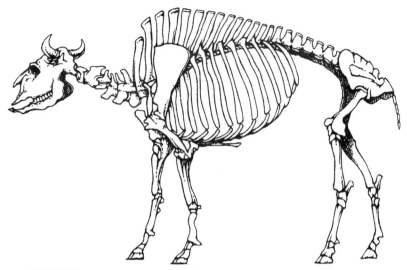

## HORNS

Both males and females are horned. Male horns are often thicker and curve upward. The largest horns recorded spanned over 35 inches, tip to tip. Female horns are more slender and sometimes have a slight backward curve. Bison do not shed their horns. The horn sheath is jet black, composed of keratinous material growing over the bony horn core. Bison use their horns for self-defense, to establish dominance in the herds, and to groom themselves.

## FUR

Calves are born with red or rusty tan fur that darkens after their first summer. As a bull ages, its coat usually gets lighter.

Winter coats are dark and thick. Summer coats are thin, with loose tufts from the shedding winter coat.

Wood buffalo are typically darker than plains buffalo.

## SPEED

Adult bison can run as fast as 38 miles per hour, nearly as fast as thoroughbred horses. They can maintain a running pace for up to 5 miles.

Calves can walk with the herd within four hours of birth.

## SENSES

Bison have poor eyesight and can see only close objects clearly. They possess a keen sense of hearing, which enables them to detect predators as well as the grunts, bellows, and snorts of other bison. Bison also have a strong sense of smell and are said to be able to detect the scent of a horse or human a mile away.

## SOUNDS

Bison communicate with low groans as they feed, particularly at night. Cows and calves vocalize with soft grunts and snorts. During the rut, males bellow frequently, a sound that can carry for miles.

## BODY LANGUAGE

Buffalo raise their tails when they are perturbed and when they defecate. Experienced naturalists warn, "When the tail goes up, they charge—or discharge."

Males also gesture aggression with head swings and foot pounding.

Bison usually face toward danger. During the winter, they stand facing into the wind.

Combative Posture

Defecation Posture

Mild Excitement

Great Excitement

## LIFE SPAN

Wild bison rarely live longer than 12 to 15 years. Managed bison live up to 20 years.

## FEEDING

Bison have no upper incisors. To eat, they seize tufts of grass with a twisting motion between their lower teeth and tongue, tearing the grass leaves and stems from the plant. This crops the grass at just about a half inch above the ground and promotes the growth of new shoots in the plant.

Bison are ruminants, meaning that they digest food in a four-chambered stomach before nutrients pass into the intestine and bloodstream. This adaptation allows them to digest tough cellulose thoroughly for maximum nutritional value. It also enables them to "eat and run." That is, they can forage in areas where they are vulnerable to predation and then digest the food when they are better protected. Like cattle, bison regurgitate food back into their mouths for extended chewing.

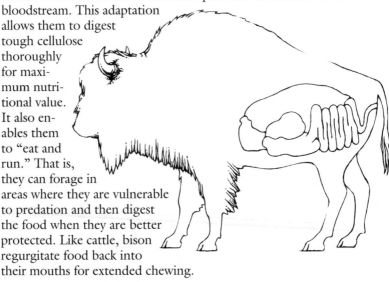

Bison usually drink once a day.

To supplement their diet, bison occasionally eat mineral-rich soil.

## PREDATORS

Humans have hunted bison since the ice age. Grizzlies occasionally prey on live bison, but more frequently they eat winter-killed carcasses. Wolves hunt bison in Wood Buffalo and Yellowstone National Parks, usually culling weak animals.

# Life in the Herd

Bison are highly social animals whose harsh environment requires them to be constantly on the move in search of food. Before the 1800s, bison apparently migrated over ranges perhaps a hundred miles in extent. Typical herd size was between 60 and 100 animals, although herds often blended with one another during their seasonal wanderings. Early observers reported seeing tens of thousands of bison in seasonal movements, but experts doubt that such vast groups constituted actual herds. Some regular patterns of migration were probably established between good grass on summer ranges and relative shelter on forested winter ranges, and between droughty plains and river valleys.

Unlike species whose social order is established by the control of territory, bison establish status in their herds by dominating one another. This can be seen in the violent threats and conflicts among males, in the control cows exercise over calves, and in the leadership of older cows, who guide the movements of cow-calf herds.

During most of the year, bison are divided into small bands of bulls and larger herds of cows. These groups may stay miles apart or drift together. Within the bull groups, individuals are scattered and independent. Except during the rut, dominance among bulls is rarely tested and individuals seem indifferent to one another. Cow herds, on the other hand, are larger, more closely knit, and have distinct leaders, usually older and larger cows.

Calving begins in April and runs well into May. This coincides with the spring "green-up" on the plains, when tender new shoots push through the withered remains of last year's grasses. A calf's birth causes only a brief pause in the perpetual movement of the herd. The pregnant cow usually leaves the herd to give birth. When the calf emerges, it is covered with a membrane, which the cow eats as she licks the calf clean. Within an hour, the calf awkwardly rises, tottering at first but rapidly gaining steadiness. Within a few hours, it can walk on its spindly legs and begin exploring the cow's underside in search of its first meal. As the calf suckles, the mother continually licks it, cementing their bond with frequent contact and murmuring sounds.

By day's end, cow and calf rejoin the herd. Other animals sniff the newcomer, but imprinting between the cow and calf has established the most important bond—the cow's strong protective instinct, which will see the youngster through its perilous first year. Cows and calves exchange low grunts to signal distress or to locate each other after brief separation. Within a month or so, the herd's new mothers form "babysitting" groups, keeping the calves enclosed within the herd and guarding them from danger.

During this time, the herd continues to wander in search of fresh sources of grass, water holes, desirable wallows, mineral licks, and protection from weather. Bison are grazers, feeding almost entirely on grasses, sedges, and rushes. In areas of good forage, they are very particular, avoiding most broad-leaved herbs and eating only the most succulent grasses. Unlike cattle, they do not overeat when food is abundant.

The ruminant's cycle of alternate grazing and digesting forms a daily pattern. Bison graze around the clock, stopping between meals for several hours to digest food (a process called "loafing"). When the herd pauses to loaf, animals scatter randomly, some lying down, some standing, as they chew their cud. Gradually, one or more rise and begin to eat in place. As an older, dominant cow moves off, others follow, continuing to feed. Known as "wave feeding," this process can carry the group three or four miles within a few hours.

At the first sign of danger, the herd mobilizes, marching in single file along well-worn single-strand or braided trails. Over the

centuries, these buffalo trails have created a filigree of hoofprint-scarred byways through the grasslands of the Great Plains.

Among themselves, bulls carry out similar cycles of feeding and loafing, but away from the crowd. Without the competition of the cow herd, bulls can be more selective in their feeding, thus getting higher-quality forage. Bull grounds are often marked by large wallows and barkless tree trunks used as scratching posts.

Mating season begins in July and ends in August or early September. Because of social dominance among males, most breeding involves males seven to eight years old, even though both males and females are sexually mature by age three. During mating season, bulls abandon their outposts to join the cows.

For a sexually mature male, the rutting season is a six-week campaign of exhausting offensive and defensive actions. The bulls test one another by charging, kicking, butting, bellowing, and bluffing. They wallow and urinate more frequently, paw and horn the ground, and raise dust clouds when startled or challenged. Mature bulls have been known to lose 200 pounds from these exertions. Although death among feuding bulls is rare, aggression is an important part of herd life.

Mingling with the cows, individual bulls "tend," or position themselves close to and move in a synchronized manner with females,

often nudging the cows in one direction or another. Periodically, the male will sniff or taste the female's rear, reacting with a gesture known as a "lip curl," in which he raises his chin and rolls his upper lip backward, often emitting a bellow. This action can attract other suitors, tiring the original bull into abandoning the female. Females often resist these overtures by walking away or butting the bull.

As the rutting season passes, bulls drift back to their outposts, and cow herds break into smaller groupings. Late-summer drought may mean that they stay closer to water sources or migrate considerable distances to new ones.

With winter snow comes the best evidence of the bison's ability to endure harsh conditions. Seemingly oblivious to blowing and drifting snow, bison nuzzle the ground, nimbly picking matted grasses as deep as three feet in the snow. A bad winter may eliminate a significant portion of the herd. Young bison, especially, fare badly. In the most demanding environments, like Yellowstone, only half the calves born in a single year survive their third winter.

Spring thaw always reveals some winterkill in buffalo country. Young and old succumb not only to the elements but also to predators such as the wolf and grizzly, and then to scavengers like the coyote, raven, and magpie. For the bison who survive, the cycle begins again in the spring.

# The World of Bison

To understand bison requires knowing their environment. Buffalo emerged from the last ice age as creatures ideally suited to life on the Great Plains. Every aspect of their physical form and social behavior was shaped by that environment. Yet, over the centuries, they helped shape that environment too. Their hooves loosened and aerated the sod, their manure and carcasses enriched the soil, and their grazing patterns maintained healthy stands of diverse grasses and herbs. Spring rains filled their wallowing pits, creating tiny wetland habitats.

The Great Plains covers about 1.5 million square miles, bounded by the Mississippi River valley on the east, the Rocky Mountains on the west, the lowlands of coastal Texas in the south, and the glacial lakes and forests of Canada's Northwest Territories in the north. This vast domain once formed the heart of buffalo country.

To early travelers, the Great Plains was a vast and hostile barrier to their journey west. Accounts depicted it as the "Great American Desert," a bleak and useless country of harsh winters, wild animals, threatening Indians, and monotonous seas of undulating grass. In reality, the Great Plains sustained a multitude of life forms, in numbers that defied calculation—from the microscopic communities living in the pores of the soil itself, to North America's largest land mammal, the bison.

Prior to white settlement, the Great Plains supported three broad types of grassland communities: the tallgrass prairie, the mixed-grass prairie, and the shortgrass prairie. All three were home to the bison. Today, most have been completely transformed by agriculture and development, but the conditions that produced them remain.

The original tallgrass prairie occupied what is now the "corn belt" of the Midwest. Many areas now dominated by corn originally supported big bluestem, a hardy perennial bunchgrass that grew to 12 feet. Rainfall in tallgrass regions averages 28 inches per year. Soils are loose, deep, moist, and nutrient-rich.

The mixed-grass prairie community occupies the mid-plains. It was the richest bison habitat. Annual rainfall here is between 14 and 23 inches, meaning less soil moisture and less organic material within the soil. The harsher, more variable climate results in more competition among grass species, and more variation in the height of plants; hence the name "mixed-grass." Fire, too, plays an important role in the mixed-grass prairie, and today, land managers who maintain native grasslands use fire as one of their most important restoration tools. Species in mixed-grass communities range in height from less than 12 inches to over 6 feet.

From the mid-plains to the Rockies, annual rainfall dwindles to about 10 inches a year. This windswept landscape is what is known as the high Plains, home of the shortgrasses. Soils here hold less water and considerably less organic material. Even "dominant" grasses such as buffalo grass can be patchy. It was the shortgrass prairies, particularly of central Montana, that saved the bison. Swept off the mid-plains by hunters and homesteaders, bison found refuge in remote pockets of range where harsh weather and isolation postponed settlement.

Today, most of the Great Plains has been dramatically and irrevocably altered. In a few places, however, grasslands have been restored and healthy herds of free-range bison maintained. (For a complete listing of where to see bison in their natural habitat, see "Bison Viewing Areas," page 39.) In these places, you can see finely integrated habitats of grasses, herbaceous plants, and trees, supporting insects, birds, rodents, jackrabbits, deer, pronghorn, elk, wolf, grizzlies—and bison. Seeing buffalo in these places is like stepping back in time to when all the Great Plains was buffalo country. On close inspection, these places show the effects of bison, including plant and animal community composition, signs of rubbing and wallowing, and the ever-present buffalo chip.

## EFFECTS OF GRAZING

When bison graze, they move constantly in scattered groups that never denude the prairie. The patchiness of their grazing creates a mosaic among the grassland communities, favoring not only a rich mix of grass species but many soft-leafed herbs, such as wild bergamot and prairie coneflower.

As bison eat, they tear leaves of grass from the plant, usually just above a "crown" at the stem base, which remains anchored firmly by deep root systems. New grass shoots quickly sprout. Bison grazing promotes vigorous new growth in the grass plant.

## RUBBING POSTS

Bison frequently rub against trees, rocks, or anything that can withstand their full weight and brute strength. Plains explorers reported seeing large boulders scattered on the plains, surrounded by depressions made by generations of bison, pausing for a satisfying scratch. In forested areas, such as Yellowstone National Park, lone bulls often rub against tree trunks and, as the rut approaches, violently spar with tree bases. Early in the summer, as bison shed their winter coats, rubbed trees are festooned with great tufts of bison fur. In the days of the telegraph, service across the Great Plains was often interrupted by bison who used the poles as rubbing posts. According to one account, when telegraph operators placed spikes in the poles to discourage the buffalo from rubbing, the animals chose those poles as their favorites.

## BUFFALO CHIPS

For all the bison's efficiency at converting grass to flesh, large amounts of food don't become buffalo at all, but are converted into manure or "buffalo chips." Buffalo chips vary from woody brown clumps to flat green disks, depending on the moisture content of the animal's food. When the bison have ingested mineral-rich soils to get the natural salts and minerals, the buffalo chips are red. In the course of grazing, a bison may roam for several miles, depositing the red chips, with their minerals and nutrients, afar.

Buffalo chips are whole civilizations unto themselves, teeming with adult and larval insects, worms, molds, and fungi. The dung beetle, or tumblebug, a relative of Egypt's sacred scarab, lays its egg in a ball of buffalo dung. Safely enclosed in its edible house, the egg hatches into a grub that then eats its surroundings.

On the treeless plains, the lowly chip was a major fuel source for Plains Indians, explorers, and early homesteaders. Dry, the buffalo chip is a portable source of energy, comparable to peat, that burns hot, with little smoke. Chips were abundant, light in weight, and required no ax to break or split. One historian joked that the buffalo chip was as important to the settlement of the West as the steam engine.

## WALLOWS

Bison habitat is often cratered with dusty pits. These wallows are where bison

roll in dust to dislodge insects from their fur. Bulls also use wallows for displays of aggression, such as pawing or horning the ground. Some bulls mark wallows with the strong scent of urine, and then roll in the mixture to coat themselves with the odor. Since the bison's hump makes it impossible to roll over completely, it rolls to either side to cover its entire back with dust.

Wallows provide habitat for other species. Seeds in the bison's coat are dislodged in wallows. The bare, loose soil provides an ideal bed for new plants. During the wet spring season, wallows fill with water and become small ponds, supporting amphibians, insects, birds, and other mammals. Look for wallows wherever there are bison.

## BUFFALO TRAILS

Bison habitat is laced with networks of paths. These bison trails are created by small herds moving in single file away from danger, led by a dominant cow or bull. Prominent trails represent decades of wear and usually mark strategic passageways near river fords, up or down steep hillsides, or through narrow ravines. Look for bison trail networks in Yellowstone's Hayden and Lamar Valleys.

## BUFFALO BIRDS

Grazing or loafing bison are often accompanied by small flocks of dark birds so predictably seen with bison that they are known as "buffalo birds." The buffalo bird is actually the brown-headed cowbird, common to open lands throughout North America. From their perching place on the bison's bony back, cowbirds dive to the ground, catching the insects disturbed by the bison's movement. Cowbirds in turn perform a service by eating flies that buzz around the bison's face and hindquarters, and occasionally foraging in the fur for parasites.

## PRAIRIE DOGS

Native grasslands throughout the Great Plains once supported as many as 5 billion prairie dogs. Sprawling "dogtowns," some hundreds of acres in extent, were aided by the presence of bison. Prairie dogs feed on grass, but prefer tender shoots of grass that have been nipped off by grazers. Good examples of dogtowns are found in Wind Cave, Badlands, and Theodore Roosevelt National Parks.

# Plains Indians and the Bison

"Plains Indians" is a collective term used to refer to the many and diverse tribes who for centuries inhabited the Great Plains and neighboring regions. These tribes included the Mandan, Missouri, Pawnee, Sioux, and Wichita of the eastern plains; the Arapaho, Teton-Sioux, Crow, Blackfoot, Cheyenne, and Comanche of the western plains; the Plains Cree, Plains Ojibwa, Shoshone, and Caddo from beyond the western edge; and, from the intermountain plateaus, the Flathead, Kutenai, Nez Perce, and San Poils.

Although vastly different in language, culture, lifeways, and geographic origins, these various peoples had in common a remarkable and complex relationship with the North American bison. All depended to some extent on the buffalo for food, fuel, tools, clothing, and shelter. Most also found in the buffalo inspiration for sacred objects, dances, songs, visions, and aspirations. Even the social organization of the tribes was shaped by buffalo—from the holy men and women who had the power to attract the herds, to the leaders who planned and organized the hunt, to the hunters who made the kill, to the villagers who skinned, butchered, and preserved the kill.

Over generations, the buffalo hunt evolved dramatically. Early Plains Indians organized into small bands that followed the seasonal migrations of bison and other prey. Such a nomadic life called for portable dwellings and few material possessions. Like their ice age ancestors, early Plains Indians hunted buffalo using projectiles such as lances or arrows, or by clubbing an animal that was swimming, or foundering in mud or deep snow.

Many tribes used "surrounds," or log corrals, to enclose small herds of bison for slaughter. The surround site was carefully selected to make the best use of the topography. The people prepared the enclosure so buffalo entered by descending a short slope. Holy men and women recognized for their ability to communicate with bison drew the animals toward the trap. Meanwhile, hunters lay in wait behind cairns, brush piles, or other small blinds along the drive route. When the buffalo approached, the hunters diverted the animals into a narrowing funnel of blinds and natural obstacles. As the bison became agitated, they moved deeper into the trap. Some fell and were injured or trampled by those behind them as the animals stampeded into the surround. The people blocked the exit and killed the animals from all sides with projectiles and clubs.

In some locations, this technique was used to drive bison over cliffs. Excavations at several sites reveal carnage on a grand scale as well as nearby camps where "industrial"-scale skinning, butchering, and drying occurred. At sites such as Madison Buffalo Jump, Montana, and Head-Smashed-In, Alberta, excavations show that killings took place periodically over hundreds of years. Archaeologists have found the remains of hundreds of animals, forming deposits 20 feet deep.

The adoption of the horse by the Plains Indians dramatically increased the hunters' mobility, giving them a new advantage over the bison. Horses were first introduced by the Spanish in about 1600; in 1800, Lewis and Clark found them abundant on the plains. As the Indian horse herds increased, so too did the hunters' range, their numbers, and the use of the horse in other aspects of tribal life.

Even after the arrival of firearms, horse-mounted buffalo hunters preferred to use traditional tools for the hunt. Astride a trained and experienced horse and armed with a short bow and 50 arrows, an expert could loose a steady stream of arrows on the run. As the pony neared the buffalo, the hunter would shoot an arrow between the animal's ribs and deep into its vital organs.

## BUFFALO PRODUCTS

Following the kill, the hunters were joined by others from the band to skin, butcher, dry, and otherwise convert the buffalo carcass to food and other items needed for daily life. These products would tide the village over until the next encounter with the wandering herds of buffalo.

When bison were plentiful and hunting good, an adult Indian subsisted on about three pounds of meat each day. Delicacies such as fresh liver and the "hump rib" were often eaten raw. Other fresh meat was roasted or boiled in containers made from rawhide or from the bladders of internal organs. Marrow, tongue, intestines, kidneys, and liver were also eaten. Blood was used for puddings and soups.

Buffalo meat was also preserved as jerky, which would retain its food value for up to three years and could be eaten dry or lightly roasted. More compact was pemmican, a pulverized jerky mixed with fat, marrow, and dried berries. Packed in a rawhide bag and sealed with hot tallow, pemmican was a dense, nutritious, portable food that could last, according to some sources, up to 30 years.

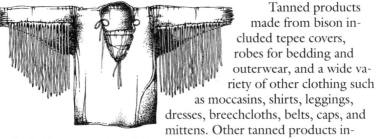

Tanned products made from bison included tepee covers, robes for bedding and outerwear, and a wide variety of other clothing such as moccasins, shirts, leggings, dresses, breechcloths, belts, caps, and mittens. Other tanned products included bags, pouches, dolls, and trade items. Tanning was demanding physical work, usually done by women. It involved handling 80-pound wet hides, tedious scraping and softening, and the deft application of tanning solutions concocted of brains, liver, and grease.

Women also made rawhide products from the buffalo. They scraped the flesh and hair off the skins and shaped products out of "green," or damp, hide. As the skin dried, it shrank and hardened, making it ideal for such items as cooking vessels, containers, moccasin soles, shields, drums, saddles, boats, masks, snowshoes, and ornaments.

Bison hair can be soft and fleecy or coarse and wiry, depending on the season and its location on the body. Hair was used to create ceremonial headdresses as well as everyday ornaments to decorate shields, tepee poles, horse tack, and clothing. Soft hair was used to pad saddles and baby carriers. Coarse hair was used to braid ropes and halters. Boiled hooves and feet were a source of glue. Unprocessed, they were used for rattles and as ornament.

Buffalo horns consist of a versatile material that becomes very pliable when heated. Stretched and formed, bison horns were shaped into ladles and fire carriers. With little or no alteration, they could become powder flasks, rattles, and headdress adornments.

Although some internal organs were eaten, the stomach, paunch, bladder, and intestines were often dried and used as containers. Intestines were used for stuffing sausage; the bladder to make medicine bags, buckets, cups, and water vessels. The stomach contents were used for medicine; gallstones, for pigment. The

brains and liver were cooked and then rubbed into scraped hide as tanning agents.

In a region with scant wood, bison bones were important for fashioning tools and a host of other implements, including knives, shovels, sled runners, saddle frames, clubs, scrapers, paintbrushes, and gaming dice. Skulls were used in ceremonies.

Sinew from along the buffalo's spine was one of the most useful materials taken from the bison. Scraped of fat and muscle, raw sinew was pliable and easily stripped into fine threads, ready for sewing or braiding into unbreakable cordage. Wider strips were used for adding strength and spring to bows, for hafting arrowheads to shafts, and for binding bone or wood together. As the sinew dried, it shrank, increasing the strength of the lashing.

Bison tails were used as sweat lodge switches, brushes, whips, and ornaments. Bison dung, or buffalo chips, were used as fuel, for ceremonial smoking, and in powdered form as a combination "disposable" diaper filler and baby powder.

## THE WHITE BUFFALO

Hundreds of spiritual teachings sprang from the peoples of Plains Indian tradition concerning the buffalo. The story of White Buffalo Woman is one of the most widely known.

In his famous oral account, the Oglala Sioux holy man Black Elk described the origin of the pipe as the gift of White Buffalo Woman. In his story, two young hunters met a stranger, a beautiful woman carrying a bundle. On her instructions the people of their village prepared a sacred tepee for her. As she arrived she sang, and a sweet-smelling cloud issued from her mouth. Opening her bundle, she presented a pipe to the chief. Carved on one side was a bison calf, symbolizing the Earth and all living things. "With the pipe," she said, "you pray for and with everything." She reminded the people of their connection to all living things: "You must always remember that the two-leggeds and all the other peoples who stand upon this earth are sacred and should be treated as such." Turning, she left them, went a short distance, and sat down. When she stood, she had become a bison calf. She lay down again, and this time arose as a white buffalo. Rolling to the ground again, she arose a third time as a black buffalo that turned and bowed to the four directions and vanished over a hill. The pipe became the most sacred object of Sioux religion. (As recounted in *The Sacred Pipe: Black Elk's Account of the Seven Rites of the Oglala Sioux*, by Joseph Epes Brown. University of Oklahoma Press, 1953, pp. 3–9.)

# The Great Killing

When Europeans arrived in North America, bison numbered between 50 million and 100 million. Their greatest concentration was in the Great Plains, where early reports described vast herds blanketing the prairies from horizon to horizon. According to Kansas settler William D. Street, one unbroken herd measured at least 20 miles by 60 miles—"two counties of buffaloes!" Wagon trains passed through masses of buffalo as if through a parting sea. Trains traveled alongside slowly moving herds for hours, and steamboats on the Missouri River could be delayed for days while thousands of buffalo crossed.

By 1889, the number of bison had been reduced to 1,000, their range to a few scattered habitats in the northern plains.

Whole libraries have been dedicated to the subject of westward expansion, and many books to the grim history of the decimation of bison herds. But the near-extinction of the buffalo had one major cause—overhunting, for both profit and sport. Two lesser factors contributed to the mass killing: loss of habitat, caused by the spread of settlement, agriculture, and railroads; and the deliberate killing of bison as way to subdue the Plains Indians.

Bison east of the Great Plains had virtually vanished by 1800, as settlements filled the Atlantic seaboard and Appalachian valleys. Early frontiersmen killed buffalo when they met them, as they did wolves and bears. In 1803, with Thomas Jefferson's purchase of the Louisiana Territory, thousands of settlers began pouring across the Great Plains, the heart of buffalo country. With them came the buffalo hunters, in search of hides and meat; the settlements, farms, and eventually railroads that claimed buffalo habitat; and the U.S. Army, which sought to subdue the Plains Indians. With buffalo described as being as plentiful "as fish in the sea," their extinction was simply unimaginable. Yet within 90 years, nearly every bison between the Mississippi River and the Pacific Ocean had been exterminated.

# THE BUFFALO HUNTERS

During the 1830s, with the decline in beaver skins from overhunting and the substitution of silk for beaver skins in hats, fur traders turned increasingly to buffalo hides, and to the buffalo hunters who supplied them. Tanned buffalo robes were popular in Eastern seaboard cities, and buffalo tongue and other meat products had ready markets in cities like St. Louis.

At first, Indians were the principal buffalo hunters, taking the hides to frontier outposts to trade. From there, the hides were transported to the Missouri and shipped downriver. In 1835, over 50,000 hides, mostly traded from Indians, went to market this way. On the southern plains, buffalo hides were transported overland along the Santa Fe Trail.

Westward-bound wagon trains in the 1840s brought non-Indian hunters into buffalo country. Emigrants on the Santa Fe and Oregon Trails supplied their parties with buffalo meat whenever possible. A single party of emigrants in Kansas in the 1850s killed over 300 animals. In addition, sport hunters (often wealthy aristocrats from other countries), lured west by heroic accounts of explorers, hired guides to lead them to the herds. One such party killed over 2,000 bison in a three-year expedition.

It was the commercial hunting frenzy of the 1870s and 1880s, however, that most devastated the buffalo herds. The demand for bison meat accelerated sharply with the influx of thousands of railroad construction workers. At least five transcontinental lines were being constructed across the plains, built by large, hungry gangs who fed on buffalo for a period of nearly 20 years. "Buffalo Bill" Cody, a meat hunter for a railroad company, boasted of killing 4,280 bison in less than 18 months.

Meanwhile, markets for buffalo hides boomed in Europe with the discovery of industrial processes to tan buffalo leather. Superior in strength to cowhide and supple as well, buffalo skin was ideal for the belts of factory machines. In 1872, the hide-export market employed between 1,000 and 2,000 hunters in western Kansas alone. Between 1872 and 1874, more than 1.3 million hides and 6.7 million pounds of meat were shipped by rail from the central plains states. At Fort Griffith, in north-central Texas, over 200,000 hides were shipped in the 1876–77 season. By 1878, the southern herd had been killed off. Many buffalo hunters abandoned the chase and turned to ranching cattle. Others turned to the northern herds of Wyoming and Montana.

By 1881, the Northern Pacific Railroad had reached the heart of the Montana plains, effectively opening the land to incoming hunters and outgoing buffalo skins. In 1882, 5,000 professional hunters and their skinners worked the northern range. From 50,000 to 80,000 buffalo were seen that year, crossing the Yellowstone River near the crowded camps of hunters. Within a few months, all of the animals had been killed.

Over the decades, the hunters had refined stategies of commercial killing, perfecting a technique called the "stand." The favored weapon was Sharp's Buffalo Rifle, with its distinctive 30-inch octagonal barrel and .45-caliber bore that could place a slug deep within a buffalo's organs from a distance of a quarter mile. Unlike the trigger-happy sportsmen, the professional buffalo hunter killed slowly and methodically. Approaching a herd from downwind, he would first kill a lead animal, usually a dominant cow. Then he would systematically pick off the other animals as they began to wander off or to sniff at their fallen herdmates. A good hunter could take down 100 animals in a single day, without startling the herd into a stampede. With prices at $3 per hide, a hunter could earn $6,000 in profit in a month—"three times what was paid . . . the President of the United States," as one buffalo hunter figured.

So successful was the hunt of 1882 that hunters at Miles City, Montana, equipped themselves for another good year. As they fanned across the buffalo grounds of the northern plains, they found nothing. In effect, the buffalo had been exterminated. Two hundred thousand hides had been shipped east in 1882. In 1884, the number was 300.

## HABITAT FRAGMENTATION

When the Union Pacific railroad was completed in 1869, it neatly sliced the Great Plains in two, dividing the buffalo into northern and southern herds. As railroad towns grew and as the railroads gave hunters access to buffalo territory, herds along the route retreated or were killed. Other railroad routes spread west, including the Atchison, Topeka & Santa Fe, which bisected the Kansas plains, and the Northern Pacific, which crossed North Dakota and Montana.

The rails themselves had the least impact on bison habitat. Much more lethal was the transfer of land to railroad monopolies and other land speculators. The U.S. government transferred 500 million acres of land to corporations and speculators, some of it Indian lands repossessed by the government and all of it former bison habitat. Rail access also ensured that settlers could enter the plains, turn the lush sod, and convert the native prairie to wheat and corn fields. Between 1870 and 1900, 430 million acres were settled, and 225 million acres were cultivated. As quickly as the bison were cleared, their habitat became farms or rangeland for the European-Americans' favorite grass-eater, the beef cow.

## GENOCIDE

The buffalo was perhaps an unintended casualty of the railroads and Western expansion. But U.S. military policies aimed directly at killing bison were clearly intentional. Their purpose was to clear the Great Plains of Indians; to do that, they targeted the bison, the mainstay of the Indians' existence.

During the mid-1800s, hostilities between Plains Indians and white settlers had been increasing dramatically, finally exploding into the Sioux Wars. After a string of Indian victories, including Custer's defeat at Little Big Horn in 1876, the Army flooded the region with troops and fortifications. White hide hunters grew bold under the protection of the Army. General Phil Sheridan said of the hunters: "These men have done in the last two years, and will do in the next year, more to settle the vexed Indian question than the entire regular army has done in the last thirty years. They are destroying the Indians' commissary. . . . For the sake of a lasting peace, let them kill, skin, and sell until the buffaloes are exterminated." That's just what they did.

# *Rebirth*

Within one brief century, the Great Plains had gone from numberless bison to practically no bison. But even as buffalo were being slaughtered, some voices were protesting. The first bill to save the buffalo was introduced in Congress by Representative Greenburg Fort in 1874. Approved by Congress, the measure was vetoed by President Ulysses S. Grant at the urging of Interior Secretary Columbus Delano, who wrote, "I would not seriously regret the total disappearance of the buffalo from the western prairies."

In the East, scientists and conservationists reacted with alarm when, in 1889, zoologist William Hornaday of the Smithsonian Institution published a report detailing the extent of the bison losses. Hornaday estimated that 200 bison survived in the remote valleys of Yellowstone, and another 500 isolated wood buffalo clung to survival in northern Alberta.

Protecting bison from poaching in Yellowstone National Park was becoming a serious problem. In 1894, when a poacher was captured, the incident was publicized in *Field & Stream*, attracting the attention of conservationists and Congress. Because of the outcry, Congress passed and President Grover Cleveland signed the Lacey Yellowstone Protection Act, the first federal law protecting bison and other wildlife in Yellowstone National Park.

Meanwhile, bison preservation was being championed by a few Western cattle ranchers. Michel Pablo and Charles Allard released their herd—descendants of six calves brought to the Flathead Valley in 1874 by Samuel Walking Coyote—into the hills of the Flathead Indian Reservation. Charles Goodnight of Texas, C. J. "Buffalo" Jones of Kansas, and Scotty Philip of South Dakota each developed small herds that would prove essential to bison survival. Pressured by conservationists and scientists, even the federal government changed its policies. In 1901, Congress appropriated money for acquiring buffalo to bolster the Yellowstone herd.

Public concern—and enthusiasm—for bison preservation mounted. In 1905, buffalo supporters formed the American Bison Society, naming President Theodore Roosevelt as honorary president. With the support of leading scientists and the conservationist president, the society waged an aggressive campaign to publicize the plight of the buffalo and create government policies to preserve them.

In 1907, the society experienced two setbacks. First it learned that rancher Michel Pablo, part owner of the Flathead herd, had agreed to sell his animals to the Canadian government, to stock Elk Island National Park in Alberta. Apparently, the U.S. Congress had rejected Pablo's earlier offer to sell the animals to the United States. In that same year, the governor of New York State rebuffed a society initiative to establish a herd in New York's Adirondack Mountains.

These setbacks helped the American Bison Society persuade Congress to create two national bison reserves. These sites became the National Bison Range in Moiese, Montana, and the Wichita Mountains Wildlife Refuge in Oklahoma. With small, well-publicized herds thriving, the society pressed for more land and sought out more privately owned bison to stock it. In 1913, the newly decommissioned Fort Niobrara Military Reservation in Nebraska was stocked with six private buffalo, Wind Cave National Park was stocked with animals from the Bronx Zoo, and neighboring Custer State Park was stocked with animals from the private herd of Scotty Philip. All of the herds prospered.

By 1930, North American bison numbered over 16,000. The American Bison Society had worked itself out of a job and quietly ceased its operations. The society, with its remarkable partnership between conservationists in the East and ranchers in the West, had helped make buffalo restoration a national priority in both the United States and Canada.

Today, North American bison number over 200,000, living in both public and private herds. Some are managed as livestock, kept in fenced ranges or feedlots and destined for market. Others range free in the geyser basins of Yellowstone or sedges of the Peace River Delta. Most herds fall somewhere in between. Some private herds, like those of Ted Turner's Flying D Ranch in Montana, live much like their wild forebears. Some public herds, like those of the National Bison Range, are managed like cattle, with pasture rotation, roundups, and brandings.

The vast majority of living bison are privately owned. Operations vary from intensively managed feedlots to large herds that are peaceably "wild" and attended infrequently by their owners.

The advantages of raising bison are many. In the proper habitat, bison seem to thrive on neglect. They require fewer antibiotics and less veterinary treatment than cattle. They weather harsh conditions well, make good use of range that would be marginal for cattle, and graze over broad dryland areas more evenly than do cattle. The demand side of the equation is also favorable. Health-minded consumers pay good prices for the lean red meat, and buffalo markets in North America and Europe are growing.

In North America, over 2,000 bison growers are organized into the National Bison Association, whose purpose is to promote the preservation, production, and marketing of bison.

## BUFFALO NATION

Fortunately, the relationship between the Plains Indians and the bison is not just a footnote in history. Many tribes have staked their future on successful reintegration of buffalo into tribal life. Organized as the InterTribal Bison Cooperative, more than 40 Indian tribes maintain bison herds as a way to regenerate cultural life, provide nutritious food, and promote economic sovereignty. Many tribes with small land bases are starting with a few animals, in the hope that commercial success will finance longer-term cultural and ecological restoration projects. Tribes like the Cheyenne River Sioux in South Dakota and the Gros Ventre and Assiniboin of Fort Belknap Indian Reservation in Montana have committed large areas of their reservations to bison restoration. Of more than 800 bison on the Cheyenne River Sioux reservation, about 16 are allocated each year for cultural and spiritual purposes, such as powwows and sun dances.

## BISON AS WILDLIFE

The complete extinction of wild bison was averted because 23 animals survived in a remote corner of Yellowstone National Park. This may have been the first time in history that a national park served as a biological "ark." In the decades when buffalo teetered near oblivion, public lands became more important for their survival. As seed herds were gathered to preserve wild bison, habitat was acquired upon which they could thrive. The national park idea was one approach. The national wildlife refuge, a new concept at the turn of the century, was another. As the wild herds grew, suitably large parcels of land in the United States and Canada were dedicated to their survival.

Today's public herds and the public lands that sustain them are a legacy fostered when survival of bison became a national cause—an antidote to the disgrace of their mass slaughter. Although bison are no longer endangered, wild bison and natural habitats for them remain threatened. There is still no consensus about whether bison are wildlife or domestic ranch animals.

Yellowstone herds are wild in the truest sense of the word. They are not handled, nurtured, or cropped, and their movements are not controlled. The forces that shape the populations are natural ones, not human ones. The bison remain free-roaming and unmanipulated not because of sentimentality or romanticism, but because they carry the bloodlines of the only continuously wild bison herd in the United States and are therefore genetically important.

The greatest threat facing Yellowstone bison is the controversy over brucellosis, a disease of domestic cattle. In cattle, brucellosis can kill first-born calves at birth. Eradication of the disease from cattle herds is an important goal of the cattle industry. Bison enter the picture because some Yellowstone animals carry the disease (possibly transmitted from cattle). In harsh winters, some bison leave the park to find food at lower elevations—on range used later in the year by cattle. Arguing that the Yellowstone exiles could spread brucellosis to cattle and threaten the disease-free status of Wyoming and Montana beef, livestock agents have shot buffalo outside Yellowstone. In 1997, 1,089 Yellowstone animals died in a hail of bullets not inflicted on wild buffalo since the 1880s.

On the surface, the debate appears to be about protecting the cattle industry from diseased buffalo. In reality, the issue is driven by starkly different visions of the value of bison as wildlife, the roles of federal agencies, and the nature of Western lands themselves—whether they should be managed pastures or remnants of a wild landscape. Solving the crisis requires cattle growers, conservationists, landowners, biologists, and bureaucrats to agree on ways to maintain separation between cattle and wild bison so that both survive. Otherwise, Yellowstone's wild bison will be pawns in a symbolic conflict like that a century ago, when the animals nearly became extinct.

# Viewing Bison Today

Bison are not domestic animals. They are wild and can be very dangerous. But as with other wildlife, watching them is fascinating. With practice, patience, and a naturalist's eye, you can recognize their beauty, subtle behaviors, and powerful presence in the landscape. Viewing bison in their natural habitat is like stepping back into history; it will help you gain an appreciation for North America's largest living land animal.

To make the most of your time with buffalo, consider the following tips and precautions:

- Bison are large, aggressive, fast, and unpredictable. Never get closer than 100 yards, and never presume that they are docile. As with all wildlife, never attempt to feed or touch them.

- Remain in your vehicle if you encounter bison on or near the road. Cars make good blinds, and bison aren't threatened by them.

- Afoot in open country, stay downwind of the herd. Keep a safe distance and plan an escape route if bison should move your way. Be sure to leave the bison an escape route too.

- Use binoculars or a spotting scope for a closer view. Be sure to look up periodically to check on animals that might be moving toward you.

- Bull-cow pairs and cow-calf pairs are very territorial, so don't approach them. Never approach a solitary calf; the mother cow isn't far away, and she can run very fast.

- Watch bison's tails for cues to their behavior. A frightened or angry animal raises its tail. So does one that's about to defecate.

- Look for other animals among or near bison herds. Cowbirds and hawks seek out insects or rodents that are disturbed by the bison.

- At smaller parks and wildlife refuges, ask rangers or visitor center staff for tips on locating bison herds. In many parks, herd locations are monitored through visitor reports or regular patrols.

# Bison Viewing Areas

The following parks and refuges manage bison herds for conservation and wildlife purposes. In addition to these areas, many zoos display bison, and many private bison ranches host visitors.

## PUBLIC HERDS

**1.** BADLANDS NATIONAL PARK, SOUTH DAKOTA
Between 300 and 600 bison range on 244,000 acres (380 square miles) of mixed-grass prairie on the plateaus and coulees of this drastically eroded environment. Several ancient buffalo jumps are located within the park, and prairie dogs are common.

**2.** CUSTER STATE PARK, SOUTH DAKOTA
South Dakota's largest state park supports about 1,500 bison on 72,000 acres (113 square miles) of mixed-grass and ponderosa forest. Buffalo can be seen from many of the park's roads.

**3.** ELK ISLAND NATIONAL PARK, ALBERTA
About 700 plains bison and about 350 wood bison roam on 48,000 acres (75 square miles) of aspen parkland and transitional grasslands. Elk Island is divided into two distinct fenced units. The south unit supports wood bison introduced from Wood Buffalo National Park after they appeared to be in danger of crossbreeding and disease. The north unit supports plains bison. The park also has a population of 300 to 400 moose and about 1,600 elk.

**4.** FORT NIOBRARA NATIONAL WILDLIFE REFUGE, NEBRASKA
About 400 bison inhabit 12,500 acres (about 30 square miles) of mixed ponderosa pine forest, canyon breaks, and sandhill prairies. The refuge has a visitor center and a 3.5-mile auto tour.

**5.** GRAND TETON NATIONAL PARK, WYOMING
Grand Teton National Park's herd of about 175 bison descended from Yellowstone transplants introduced in 1948 and supplemented in 1964 with buffalo from Theodore Roosevelt National Park. The bison roam on 275,000 acres (430 square miles) of mixed ponderosa pine forest and sagebrush plains, finding winter cover in the valleys of the Snake and Gros Ventre Rivers.

**6.** MACKENZIE BISON SANCTUARY, NORTHWEST TERRITORIES
This herd of about 2,000 wood bison descended from a small, isolated herd of 18 that were relocated from Wood Buffalo National Park in 1963 to prevent interbreeding with plains buffalo. The sanctu-

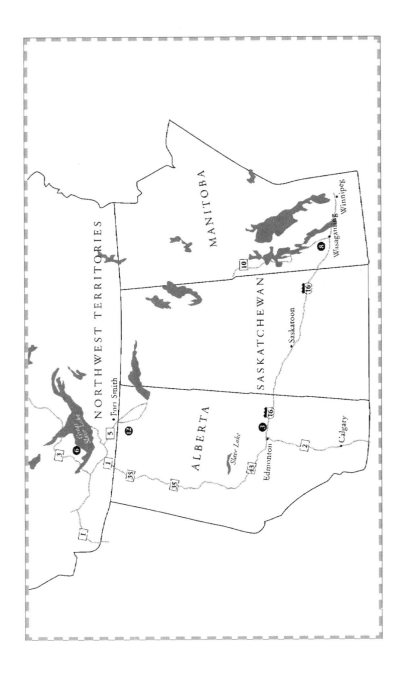

NORTHWEST TERRITORIES

MANITOBA

SASKATCHEWAN

ALBERTA

Winnipeg

Wasagaming

Saskatoon

Fort Smith

Calgary

Edmonton

Slave Lake

Great Slave Lake

10

8

16

3

16

5

12

3

6

1

2

43

35

35

1

41

ary occupies 2.4 million acres (3,860 square miles) on the western shore of Great Slave Lake.

## 7. NATIONAL BISON RANGE, MONTANA

The National Bison Range (NBR) is especially significant for its historical role in bison conservation. Range managers maintain 350 to 450 bison on 18,500 acres (29 square miles) of hilly bunchgrass prairie. Remote areas of the range are accessible by a one-way auto tour that climbs into high forests. Bison are usually visible from this road, along with elk, mountain sheep, antelope, and mule deer. NBR holds a roundup, open to visitors, on the first Monday and Tuesday of each month.

## 8. RIDING MOUNTAIN NATIONAL PARK, MANITOBA

The Riding Mountain herd was created in 1931 from descendants of Michel Pablo's Flathead Valley herd. Riding Mountain maintains a small herd of 30 bison on 980 acres (1.5 square miles) of bunchgrass prairie and aspen parkland forest. Bison and their habitat are interpreted with displays and roadside viewing.

## 9. THEODORE ROOSEVELT NATIONAL PARK, NORTH DAKOTA

Located on the western edge of North Dakota, Theodore Roosevelt National Park is composed of rugged badlands, mazelike coulees, and river-bottoms. The South Unit, just outside Medora, supports 300 bison on 46,000 acres (72 square miles). The North Unit, about 50 miles north of Medora, supports 100 bison on 24,000 acres (38 square miles).

## 10. WICHITA MOUNTAINS NATIONAL WILDLIFE REFUGE, OKLAHOMA

This refuge along the remains of an ancient mountain range maintains a herd of about 500 bison on 60,000 acres of mixed-grass prairie and post oak forest. The refuge also supports a herd of 500 longhorn cattle. There is a campground, a visitor center, and hiking trails.

## 11. WIND CAVE NATIONAL PARK, SOUTH DAKOTA

Situated in the southern Black Hills, Wind Cave National Park maintains about 300 bison on 28,500 acres (about 45 square miles) of mixed-grass prairie and ponderosa pine. Originally created to protect a vast system of limestone passages and caverns with rare and delicate formations, Wind Cave was enlarged to support bison. Despite the attraction of the cave, many visitors come to see bison, prairie dogs, and the Black Hills' finest stands of mixed-grass prairie. The park has a campground, a visitor center, and many miles of trail.

**12.** WOOD BUFFALO NATIONAL PARK, ALBERTA AND NORTHWEST
TERRITORIES
The world's second-largest national park was created in 1922 to
protect about 1,500 wood bison that survived in this remote region
of Canada. Today, the park is home to between 2,500 and 3,000
bison, mostly hybrids of plains and wood bison. The park includes
11.1 million acres (17,375 square miles) of mixed habitats, including spruce-aspen forests and river-delta wetlands of sedge and willows.
The park's remoteness and scale preserves the predator-prey relationship between wolves and bison. Both are reported to be the
largest of their respective species. Wood Buffalo National Park is
also a breeding habitat for the extremely rare whooping cranes.

**13.** YELLOWSTONE NATIONAL PARK, WYOMING AND MONTANA
The crown jewel of national parks and bison conservation, Yellowstone supports the only free-roaming and unmanipulated bison
in the United States. About 2,000 bison inhabit 2.2 million acres
(3,458 square miles) of lodgepole pine forest and sedge meadows.
Herds are mostly found in Hayden, Lamar, Pelican, and Firehole
Valleys. Yellowstone's geothermal features form crucial winter habitat for bison, providing pockets of refuge where lighter snowpack
means easier feeding and movement for the animals. Wildlife viewers
have abundant opportunities to observe not only bison but also
antelope, deer, elk, grizzly and black bears, moose, coyotes, and
recently reintroduced gray wolves.

## TRIBAL HERDS

**14.** FORT BELKNAP INDIAN RESERVATION, MONTANA
The Gros Ventre and Assiniboin Tribes of Fort Belknap Agency
have restored a herd of about 300 bison to 10,000 acres of shortgrass prairie. Visitors may view the bison on guided tours led by
tribal members, who also share their knowledge of other wildlife,
important plants, and Plains Indian tradition.

**15.** INTERTRIBAL BISON COOPERATIVE
Visitors are welcome on several reservations of InterTribal Bison
Cooperative (ITBC) member tribes. Programs and visitor services
are limited because of staff and facilities. For more information
about specific ITBC member tribes and their educational programs,
contact ITBC, PO Box 8105, Rapid City, SD 57709-8105.

## PRIVATE HERDS

**16.** NATIONAL BISON ASSOCIATION

The association represents 2,100 bison ranchers in 50 states and 16 countries. It promotes raising and marketing bison and bison products and provides technical assistance to its members and potential bison growers. It maintains a bloodline registry and holds annual bison auctions. The association also provides information about visitor services offered by its members. Contact the National Bison Association, 4701 Marion St., Suite 100, Denver, CO 80216.

**17.** TALLGRASS PRAIRIE PRESERVE, THE NATURE CONSERVANCY, OKLAHOMA

About 650 bison range on 8,600 acres of restored tallgrass prairie in Oklahoma's Flint Hills. Eventually, the Nature Conservancy herd will reach about 2,000 animals and use up to 90 percent of the preserve's 37,000 acres. Bison and prescribed fire are the principal tools being used to restore this fragment of tallgrass prairie, which includes 8-foot-high big bluestem, Indiangrass, and switchgrass, as well as about 500 other plant species. Visitors can hike, picnic, or drive through the site on an auto-tour route.

# Resources

## BOOKS AND ARTICLES

Berry, Willia. *Buffalo Land*. Press North America, 1988.

Brown, Joseph Epes. *The Sacred Pipe: Black Elk's Account of the Seven Rites of the Oglala Sioux*. University of Oklahoma Press, 1953.

Brown, Lauren. *Grasslands*. Alfred Knopf, 1985.

Callenbach, Ernest. *Bring Back the Buffalo! A Sustainable Future for America's Great Plains*. Island Press, 1996.

Dary, David. *The Buffalo Book: The Full Saga of the American Animal*. Sage Books, 1974.

Foster, John, et al. *Buffalo*. University of Alberta Press, 1994.

Grinnell, George Bird. "The Last of the Buffalo." *Scribner's Magazine*, September 1892.

Guthrie, R. Dale. *Frozen Fauna of the Mammoth Steppe*. University of Chicago Press, 1990.

Haines, Francis. *The Buffalo: The Story of American Bison and Their Hunters from Prehistoric Times to the Present*. University of Oklahoma Press, 1995.

Hornaday, William. "The Extermination of the American Bison, with a Sketch of Its Discovery and Life History." Report of the U.S. National Museum, 1887.

Johnston, Ruth. *The Buffalo Cookbook*. Hancock House, 1995.

Manning, Richard. *Grassland*. Penguin Books, 1995.

McDonald, Jerry. *North American Bison: Their Classification and Evolution*. University of California Press, 1981.

McHugh, Tom. *The Time of the Buffalo*. Alfred Knopf, 1972.

Meagher, Mary. "Bison," in *Big Game of North America*, Schmidt and Gilbert, eds. Stackpole Books, 1979.

Meagher, Mary. "Winter Weather as a Population-Regulating Influence on Free-Ranging Bison in Yellowstone National Park." *Research in the Parks*. National Park Service, 1976.

Peacock, Doug. "The Bison Massacre: A Report from Yellowstone." *Audubon Magazine*, June 1997.

Pickering, Robert. *Seeing the White Buffalo*. Denver Museum of Natural History, 1997.

Rau, Violet. *American Buffalo: The General Store for the Indians of the Great Plains.* Celia Totus, 1992.

Sample, Michael. *Bison: Symbol of the American West.* Falcon Press, 1987.

Shult, Milo. *Where Buffalo Roam.* Badlands Natural History Association, 1979.

Taylor, Dave. *The Bison and the Great Plains.* Crabtree Publishing, 1990.

## ORGANIZATIONS

Greater Yellowstone Coalition
13 S. Willson, PO Box 1874
Bozeman, MT 59715

InterTribal Bison Cooperative
PO Box 8105
Rapid City, SD 57709-8105

National Bison Association
4701 Marion St., Suite 100
Denver, CO 80216

# The Sasquatch Field Guide Series

*Nifty little guidebooks with good graphics, easy reading, and solid scientific facts.*

"The best buy in natural history reading available."
—Charlie Powell, Outdoor Columnist, *Moscow-Pullman Daily News*

**TITLES IN THE SASQUATCH FIELD GUIDE SERIES:**

The Greater Yellowstone Coalition
**Field Guide to the North American Bison**

The Oceanic Society
**Field Guide to the Gray Whale**

The Audubon Society
**Field Guide to the Bald Eagle**

Adopt-a-Stream Foundation
**Field Guide to the Pacific Salmon**

Great Bear Foundation
**Field Guide to the Grizzly Bear**

Oceanic Society Expeditions/Earthtrust
**Field Guide to the Humpback Whale**

Western Society of Malacologists
**Field Guide to the Slug**

People for Puget Sound
**Field Guide to the Geoduck**

International Society of Cryptozoology
**Field Guide to the Sasquatch**

American Cetacean Society
**Field Guide to the Orca**

*Each field guide in this series helps support a non-profit foundation dedicated to the conservation of natural habitats and species. The cover design and illustration are by award-winning nature illustrator Dugald Stermer.*

SASQUATCH FIELD GUIDES ARE AVAILABLE FROM YOUR LOCAL
BOOKSTORE OR CALL TOLL FREE 800-775-0817.

**SASQUATCH BOOKS**
**SEATTLE**
www.sasquatchbooks.com